WEST

WEST

WEST

GIORDANO DURANTE

Published by The Dabuti Collective

ISBN: **1999887603**

ISBN13: **9781999887605**

This debut collection starts with a series of poems about Gibraltar. "Alameda Interlude", one of the most ambitious works here, ties together historical reflection and autobiographical reminiscence.

The second section looks at Andalucía and its cities. Durante examines the bizarre rituals of Catholicism and the emotional tug they still exert in "Semana Santa" and "Folklore".

The third section inhabits the metropolitan gloom of London and contains the title poem "West" and meditations on the unacknowledged beauty of the "unloved" towns and suburbs.

The final section – a ragbag of pieces which don't fit comfortably into the previous classifications – contains the deeply personal "Katie" and "Ghost Train", a tribute to a fairground entertainer.

'The business of the poet and the novelist is to show the sorriness underlying the grandest things and the grandeur underlying the sorriest things.'

Thomas Hardy

CONTENTS

WEST

NOTE

I need to thank my parents for bringing me up in a house surrounded by volumes of Hopkins, Hardy and Heaney. Echoes of these poets (and others) resonate through this collection.

My deepest gratitude goes to my father who filled my life with verse, passed on his love of words and drew my attention to what was worth celebrating in a poem.

I also need to thank Lorraine for her patience and for putting up with me getting up at 5am in order to write and polish this collection.

I am very grateful to M.G. Sanchez for reading a proof and guiding me through the publishing process.

Thanks also go to Stefano for speedy logo work.

PART ONE

BISHOP CANILLA HOUSE

These lace curtains sieve the smell of cabbage from a bubbling
potaje;

Maruja's vegetables and cheap beef cuts mix with the odour of
bleach.

Terrier piss stains the street outside –

A match for the occasional incontinence within.

Mario's arthritic hand ineptly holds the first cigarette of the day,

The nicotine rush will soon make him dizzy.

He'll lie down now and wait for the buxom help to arrive with
cakes from Morrison's and the lottery.

Maribel watches the same soaps every afternoon.

Hard of hearing, the stilted Mexican exchanges blare out into the
corridor.

She's 89, or so she thinks, and often recalls her time in Kingston

During the evacuation and that ripped Rastafarian she bedded.

Adela and Aurelio's dried lips meet – "Buenos días mi amor"

They say as they empty their heavy catheters.

Nestled next to his pancreas, a growth the size of a fist

And her tired arteries have begun their final narrowing.

And my flesh sags

And numbness spreads across my limbs

So I shuffle from bed to sofa cutting through a humid afternoon,

And wake to the bald terror of the canary's song.

GABRIEL MORENO

Mustachioed troubadour

Who, in Hull, breathed in Larkin's lines;

Who, in Barcelona, dreamt of London

And conjured Lorca's olive groves

In a wet November traffic jam.

AULD LANG SYNE

I've drained this eve to its very lees

Till all that's left is gimcrack entertainment

To bolster our manufactured gin-joy

Old acquaintance never showed up

So I lie still in bed

We must spend more per capita

On fireworks than any other nation –

Can I use this boast one day?

The bangs bring to mind the chaos

Of street battles

A brochure might say: "Enjoy the thrill of Aleppo

From your cosy council flat."

But this, our calculated, arbitrary cheer

Calendar-directed, in multiple flashes,

In a cloud of party-popper sulphur,

Sounds hollow this year

The men with paunches still wave sparklers

And proudly supervise suburban pyrotechnics

Rekindling perhaps their torrid teens

In a plot involving Prosecco and gunpowder

But not me

For I am like an idle, deranged lord

And wake up in a silence at six

To survey its total grip

On this anaemic morning

I do have this one perverse pleasure, though:

To watch the town sleep through till lunch

While, in this order, I set out

The year's ingredients: eggs, coffee

And a book on Heidegger.

HOWL [FOR GIBRALTAR] (1991)

I saw the best minds of my generation destroyed by smuggling, bloated gold-covered half-mad,

running across beaches and black warehouses at dawn dragging boxes, bales and flares,

mullet-headed *chulo putas* smoking high grade weed…

MAHOGANY

At the reception,

Surrounded by the musty

Relics of our

Colonial masters,

Fed by dry canapés,

Watered by plonk in plastic cups,

We enter this spinning

Midday purgatory.

I should have

Been a randy mouse

Scuttling under these

Wooden floors

Instead, I fidget in a corner.

Is it too early

To make a shrouded exit?

The speech ended,

We "mill"

Reaffirm tacit social rank

Like Macaques inspecting

Their plum arses.

Some lawyer-jerk comes

And bores me, misidentifies me

For the tenth time

While already eyeing the high-powered

Blonde who's just walked in

All shoulder pads and Gucci scent.

And now a charitable do-gooder

Who's cheating on his sick wife,

The spineless journalist,

The swindling contractor,

And the bouffant-haired son

Of the tobacco cartel.

Such voluntary obsequiousness.

"Ladies and gentlemen"

I do not announce my retreat.

I'll leave these phantoms to

Their clumsy bump and grind.

I shun the bitchy, chattering classes

To seek a form of glory in

The contents of my mind.

BOULEVARD

Nothing like the brotherhood

Of a midnight piss among friends;

Our aureate streams slowing to a dribble

Between the iron railings.

Then, on Friday nights, overlooking

Prefab houses with their dingy kitchens

Lined with worn cloths,

We took temporary ownership

Of the garrison; its roaming cats.

Now, re-scaled by work and wife

And hypochondria, tending swinging children,

We gaze at yet more foundations

For luxury flats with perhaps

A lingering longing for the old.

ALAMEDA INTERLUDE

Once struck,

With a furtive cluck

The day begins;

Dragon tree, stone pine, succulents,

Bougainvillea and fanning palms

All suck the early light

Into their earthy essence.

If it were August, the cicada would be

Proclaiming her noisy rule. Instead,

In that life-humming tree, a dove

Softly speaks her three-note demotic.

It was here that, as children,

We straddled the fat cannon,

Rode them like rockets,

Here that a solider from Lancaster,

His freckled face burnt

By this sun, posted amid the ants and

Redolent of port fumes, walking

Beyond the garrison's boundary,

(An extramural edgeland of separate rules and mores)

Turned his thoughts to 'M' back home,

Her flaxen hair and deep eyes –

Is she lying

In bed now in that stone city?

Do her unpunctuated thoughts run to him?

Words drift, flit and dodge,

And our mongrel talk

Traces your weeds

And unruly roots as they break through

Tired tarmac, openings, torn

Surfaces and hollows within bushes;

Garbled vowels floating among the

Wild olives, the throat-cry of a Mediterranean

Diaspora, like a dry western wind;

From an estate nearby, a blend of Latin tongues

And archaic colonial English

Can be heard while a fire engine sets off.

These cracked paths have seen multiple

Philanderers and piles of filth.

On this bench, we sculpted our teenage words

To tender expression and today

We witness love in all its forms:

A tattooed expat – surely a Brexiteer –

Marrying a lissom Thai bride,

Snapped for a monthly magazine.

And so, as Britain beats her slow retreat,

And her columns all that stand,

Shit-besmirched Eliott

Still gazes out, silent,

Towards a car park.

LEVANTE

Sea-flanked

Battleground for cawing gulls

And arrowhead swifts

That swim through the

Airless morning.

Grey fluff-muffled world

And the orange lights of bulk

Carriers, their bass horns

Filling the static fog;

Their superstructures

Disembodied,

Like the faraway towers

Of a city shedding its parts

To the veiled bay.

And are the bin men now showered

And in bed, fragrant

Next to waking wives,

Their eyelids heavy

With beads of sweat?

EASTERN BEACH MAN

The inept husband

Like a simple donkey

With stools and towels hanging

From every limb

Shuffles up the sand.

Everything he does

Is wrong in his wife's eyes

(She who hates the thought of sand

Touching food or towels)

From the angle of the beach umbrella

To the position of the fridge

Relative to the shifting shade

And the specific Calippo she ordered.

And all he can think,

As he pours water on the scorching sand

To create a cool path to the sea

Is that, once again, he forgot

To cover his balls in Vaseline.

MAIN STREET (for C.C)

Through this stick, the road

A tactile blueprint

Laid out like a tablecloth

On the contours of my inner dark.

A map of bumps and cracks;

Urban braille: thud, jump, blip.

Bat-like, I navigate waves –

This on the left, Copacabana,

A morning cackle from a rough regular,

And, to my right, the diesel tick

Of a delivery van.

I am also all nose;

Breathing the cigarette smoke

Of the bars, their stale beer,

And ahead, the perfumed wake

Of Tony Lombard –

So it must be half past eight.

I know my city to be different from yours −

My fragrant child, my uneven one,

How you hum.

PAVANA

Flung up, untethered,

On a quivering wing

By wind and air

Buffeted by the wild

Gust and tug that rises

From the slanting trees,

The gull dangles

Two lifeless yellow legs

Like, an hour before,

A limp, gleaming bream

Hung from its bill.

And now with a tremble the

The uncertainty of a lost kite.

PART TWO

FOLKLORE

We left the heaving, unchaste club at two

And roamed the city's cobbled streets.

Turning down a steep hill, close to *la Mezquita*,

A file of men lugging a mock float,

Their blessed Virgin just a pile of bricks.

Shuffling up the moonlit lane

With military discipline, their whispered drill

Filling the Córdoba night.

The local ashen-faced sceptic

Stopped with us to watch,

His mocking posture inviting debate or comment.

"A circus…" I ventured.

"No, just folklore," he corrected and walked off

Looking at his worn shoes.

SEVILLA

American gold and tobacco made you

Low, baked city.

Your cathedral, like some fat, sandy octopus

Looms behind every orange-blossomed corner.

In your swarming bars,

Straw-tinged *fino* is served

By men with gypsy eyes.

On the banks of your swollen river

At dusk, I might compose a southern dirge

For guitar and castanets

And dream of moonlit Mudéjar arches.

Sevilla, I forgive you your smell of horse manure.

TRENCH

You get a special kind of chill

On these hills on summer nights

When the wind from the west

Brings the smell of resting cattle

The earth and its scrawny plants

Still carry some afternoon heat;

The memory of the cicada,

Dusty bees and the lone goatherd;

Aged cheese, manure and death.

He passed at dusk on his clapped out

Motorbike, sounding like a

Fighter plane failing, falling.

That ditch we came across −

The stone pit of gorse

That surprised us so early −

Well, you claimed it was

Some trench or even a crater

From one of Franco's bombs.

The front moved across the valley,

You said, like a shadow,

And it took long

For "Red Casares" to fall

Where the men were dragged

Away and shot among the pines.

SEMANA SANTA

Two o'clock and the thud,

The swaying float

And there she is,

Bloody tears on her

Dark face,

Behind a low wall of carnations.

She looks like

The women of this neighbourhood

Who stand wet-eyed, clutching rosaries.

Atlas-like, the hundred

Bear her from

Church to fountain square

To imperfect trumpets,

Cushioned

On tracks of white, tight trainers.

Next *los novios de la muerte,*

Their triceps thrusting

Christ to the afternoon sun,

A pagan offering from the

Bearded cohort.

Blood, death, heat, the military

And gaudy Catholicism –

Andalucía, you

Are so much yourself.

MALAGA

Christ tours these streets at night,

The crowds parted by antiseptic spray;

His central home the lopsided cathedral

With its incense-clouded lances of light.

The Sunday sermon covered the puny

Logic of humans and how there are

Things that, free from grubby mercantile

Hands, simply have no price.

Down from *la manquita*,

I filled my own lack with

A plate of fluffy fried whitebait.

You wear your amelia well,

Rough, cobbled-together port with

A concrete river and towers pimpled

With air conditioning units,

And, always at the end of a street, surrounding hills of hard scrub.

PART THREE

WEST

It was a tip circulating in halls:

Take the parallel route.

Unbound and pint-filled,

Avoiding the Oxford Street rush.

With that openness to possibility

Furnished by an evening drink,

You move down Goodge Street.

The Capricorn Club's steep stairs

Lead to the grimy interior of the city.

A den of soot and rats where the men drink scotch

While their beaten, peroxide wives sip Babycham.

Nonsense! – You never entered; the gorilla outside,

Perched on a stool,

Flexed his thick knuckles.

Next door, a flour-dusted trattoria – not a chain,

But a sinking independent establishment.

The matt Chianti bottles suck in all the light;

They sit on garish, chequered tablecloths.

By Mortimer Street, the liquid sun is

Splashed across the turrets of stained buildings.

You can feel the chill of early October now

As evening sprouts a stealthy transformation.

Soon the cloaked drunks will trip over cardboard boxes

In search of a cubbyhole by a hot air vent;

Home for the night while the foxes

Reclaim the street.

Overlooking this jumble is the BT Tower;

Blue beacon of lost Somali minicab drivers.

***

Walking west on Wigmore Street

With the gleaming, glowing city

Both wobbling ahead

And subject to a kind of sharpening;

A deepening of relations.

Urban inversion of the heat shimmer.

Your heavy bladder

And onion thoughts

Embedded in this acrylic evening scene.

***

It seems an in-between, shape-shifting life,

That you've grasped unthinkingly here

As you turn left down Orchard Street;

A life without loss but ripe for it.

And now you're taking on some of that light over there.

It drains you.

It fills you so deeply.

[unfinished]

GATWICK – VICTORIA

We move ahead in spaces between fences,

The fortifications that keep office blocks and the rich safe;

The barbed wire, no climb paint, the steel spears

And hedgehog balls bristling like some torturer's play kit.

The very disorder of back gardens with their misery of unused,

Rusting trampolines –

More overspill of life's accumulated mess than green belt.

Sinking damp buildings and daily parking for £19

(a sign sprayed in the muscular letters of a local tag)

You can read the mud brown despair stretched out

Across this concrete grid half torn.

What lives lie hidden behind these filthy curtains?

What silent suffering is lit by that bald bulb?

But to ask is to project a mystery that isn't there;

To mistake the cycle of microwave meals for complexity and love.

Clapham opens out one last time before the city surrounds you

And tourists with their foreign breath fill the carriage.

MARGINS

The way people render

The smallest things

Into highlights, quests:

We would travel by car

North to that unremarkable

Town fed by a motionless canal

The retired rich had

Attracted a new brand

Of shop with unnecessary

Snacks and New World wines

Emerging with a haul of carbs

To ward off the early dark

We visited the bookshop

And browsed, expecting

Gardening books and the Famous Five

But otherwise barren shelves

But no –

Some "John Mable" had left

A bunch of books

On the mind and Wittgenstein

His careful script – all elegant

Curves with the odd flourish –

Suggested a retired miner

Schooled during evening

Classes once he had

Scrubbed the soot off his hands

With tar soap; his face glowing –

Twenty-two but with old eyes –

Had he done a distance course

In his spent years?

His puzzlement, expressed

In the margins – at some times an

Exclamation mark, at others an

Exasperated series of dots –

That of a man new to learning

Or eagerness deflated that

It all led to a beetle

In a box

With resigned patience,

He brought the raw pit

To bear on western thought

But was he perhaps seeing further,

The dark pen pressing down

On printed pulp

Pinning down absurdities,

Noting subtleties that might escape

The jaded, institutionalized eye

Naively, he often ventures

It's one huge hoax

Hatched in a basement in London

Mr Mable, sat in his semi,

Two bar electric fire going;

Outside, a gust.

Turning to a discussion

Of mental causation

The dogged autodidact

Reflects that

He has at least this brief encounter

With words that fill him with

Worry and which

One day will seal him and time

In a tomb of crumbling paper and

Mould

And he'll tumble headlong

Down the shaft, blinded by glimpses

Of gauzed light.

LETTERS TO M

You played jazz records

On those evenings of

Grey to

Muffle the drip

To give your own

Stale bachelorhood

A half-hearted squeeze

And catapult your lyrical

Longing into her pink-sweatered arms

The bridges and docks and cranes

And sad rivers of unloved towns

Contributed their own brand

Of misery and neglect

To not have written verse

Would have been unnatural

Like not going for a walk

When snowfall is rare.

MARBLE ARCH – LUTON AIRPORT

And the trees are a mist

A rough brushwork horizon

Between the empty fields

Leafless borderlands

Are all that we can bear

At this sorry time

But what is England?

A fading tapestry

Somehow still strung by one long

Convoy of lorries from

Northern factories to

Park Lane

The low afternoon sun

Exerts an elemental tug

Away from fat and grime

And chips and wrappers

And memories of hospitals.

TRIBUTE

This is for the outsourced, the sleepless, those who lie all day on dank sofas, the criminal, the liminal, the overaters and vomiters, those who pray and keep praying, those who forget to replace the toilet roll, those who smoke, who toke, who're broke, who feed themselves envy, the jealous, the arse-lickers, the slick, the sick, those who drive too quick, those whose names begin with an 'X', those who've changed their names, who've wondered what another name would do, would sound like, to all those who shiver, who watch old movies all day long, who scroll for the lols, who watch Sky News and its dizzying ticker, those with a dodgy ticker, ticket touts, louts and those who shout out at night, having forgotten their keys.

FLATLANDS

timeless light, could be afternoon

or evening,

almost night

static glow, earth's weak

orange bulb, flow of

dread birdsong through

the greying trees

a raised train line cut the back garden;

ahead, through wooden slats,

the churned fields;

either life destroyed –

ground down to useless powder –

or its very beginning in brown moisture

you were on the fringes of the London art crowd,

fleeing the competition and rising prices,

and invited the area's misfits –

the sots of local amateur dramatics,

the divorcées and those running

away from a minor disgrace –

to a party in an airless outhouse

these evenings with their air of drawn out loss,

like a thumb that forms a bruise

something changed then and was gone

no more innocence in belief and thought

and with a nightcap as the music died,

the inkling of some filthy hoax

that editor, memory, has cut

most out and made that time

a distant ache,

traces

now include a series

of paintings of light bulbs

hanging above a flat land;

a piano miniature played on a crackly LP before you rise.

PART FOUR

ODE TO AN ISLAY MALT

At first, the peaty stink;

A sea-salt swirl

Deep and rank,

It leaves its oily trail across the glass.

A certain smokiness

As if some weather-cracked hands had lit a fire,

Tool-beaten hands that speak of a screenless world.

From cask to dram,

And now a final communion of taste.

In a darkened room, my mouth plays host

To honeyed bliss.

I become the northern winds, the turf

And thistle.

Drinking is an act of reverence;

Drawn-out, contemplative.

A mouthful of sodden earth,

To earth and black pebble we shall return.

e-love

hey info

let us talk

i wish we could plan to hang out

click

without you by my side i am feeling love

i'm missing out

AUTUMN

(après Verlaine)

"there are places…whose relationship of parts creates a mystery, an enchantment, which cannot be analysed." - Paul Nash

Those autumn violins have come together

To form a melancholy quartet

And that almost solid, post-prandial light

Has entered the petal-shadowed room for let.

A light fed, it seems, through clear water

Lending it the air of your dancing child,

Our lost daughter.

Of course you had a large brandy after lunch

And now it courses through every languid limb

As you lie there speaking of Paris.

Your gravel voice offers up statements for inspection;

The dappled room frames them suspiciously within brackets.

One accusation dies quietly unnoticed,

One regret exits without commotion.

The day – no, the hour – takes on a last romantic strain,

The taut instruments slowly rising now

For a coda of unyielding despair

As colours deepen, merge and dissolve.

We're just one blue note away

From dissonant disarray.

I think I've always preferred monotony to sobs;

Held on to dead leaves and old days.

KATIE

Miniature mother to the dismembered dozen,

Fickle, fleet urchin,

Immune to the odd bump

But fragile too,

Brought down for days by a cold

Or injured by a sharp word or look.

What early thoughts fill your mind

Of a world where everyone must sleep

At your behest?

Of forbidden foods

And the dog's renegade claim to titbits,

Of corners, cubbyholes

The enchanted spaces of the young?

Your linguistic experiments

Bring snatches of song

And echoes of verbal tics

Unknown even to us.

Disheveled daughter,

Can we predict your nature

From a complex genetic sum of parts?

How can your flourishing

Be bound up in you now when

The world and

A single day contain so much

Unearned triumph and decline?

Always behind you, I pick up

A doll; its purple hair

Plucked out by your small fingers.

MEAT

A lisping priest −

        and a routine of stagnant traditions

we move on by default

whenever others make choices for us the silent

80 kilos of boxed meat and sinew

        slowly going off

sprinkled over the polished coffin

are ineffectual drops of water

        because preparing for nothingness is hard

the emaciated

onlooker up there dangling

such a pitiful, wasted figure for a god

life just gone cold

and

graveyard

sparrows and dead flowers

will mean more

why this same mould for millions

encasing spontaneous wonder

doubt and a dozen minor rebellions?

that a wanton weekend

                  the privacy of desire

and the very fullness of it all

might be cut down, packaged

§

Sparrows, scattering now

                  (their dusty, half-dead eyes

their nervous

animal innocence)

seem to know more about this

SAW

We shook on it

Fired up

The night before

And, true

To my word,

Got up on time

The small saw

With a smudge of rust

And movement

Sat in my grip

Easy, warm,

Its wooden handle worn

I hacked at

The barely conquerable

Weed-bush for hours

Its thorns dug into

My arms and shins

And hidden insects scurried

Months later, in London,

My tan faded and left

Marks – white hyphens – on my forearms.

CINEMA

The way they look out,

Superior, facing a stone courtyard

In the rain

Seen through drops which

Dapple already lightly pockmarked skin

Watching, like you, some terse neurotic tale

Uncoil through their own screen

Moody, pursed lips showing

Cracks of experience (never age)

Containing lovers (always younger) picked

Up in trains

That relaxed air of knowing

The way they push their

Fading hair from their eyes

To read or think aloud

Unschooled but intellectual,

Quoting Nabokov −

Waltzing, disastrous examples of bad faith

By night, temptresses of the demi-monde

With their dark eyelids and petite breasts;

But then posted outside schools like doleful swans

Collecting the children of absent husbands

And smoking, always smoking −

No one took a drag like you −

Here's smoking good enough

To make one smoke

Oh such noxious charm

At school, within an adolescent fug

We conjugated fruitlessly,

Unaware we could unlock all this.

BLACKBIRD

Have you seen how a blackbird

Scampers across a garden wall?

Bent low, led by his beak,

A spirit level line from

Crown to tail, hurrying

In bursts.

Balanced or weightless,

Legs blur as a freshly vacated

Bird-shaped emptiness

Follows.

They hop too, but this is better −

This suits the mystery

Of this dark mercurial presence

As he heads for the leaves

To fill my morning ear

With liquid variation.

BODY AT 36 YEARS

A small, upright,

prickly crest crowns a

hairline which

has been receding

so slowly

it's hard to see

such gentle withering

without daily

vanity.

Skin lined

by sun and

a general disposition

to frown

and look dour

but perhaps tauter

thanks to

'Bulldog' cream for MEN

A slight

blush on the

tip of the nose;

years of evening drinks.

Chest carries

the slack brawn

of prophylactic

hours at the gym.

Moving down,

below the

lint-catching whorl,

a left-leaning

slumbering digit

and so much life.

I've carried around

what carries

me in all its

shifting guises

and suffered its spasms —

unavoidably mine —

not like a pilot in his ship,

but so compounded

and intermingled.

ROAR

Silence is the expectation of noise;

The preparation for a clink at the gate,

A foot brushing through and parting leaves —

It makes a sound possible;

Empty air the prelude.

Stirring now in a burning panic

When before you'd lie

Here and sleep

Late uninterruptedly.

But this was before you

Became the paterfamilias;

Now you're that first and last

Line of domestic defence;

A crooked stick resting by the door.

That flat point when winds change,

When the westerly fades

For the squalls of tomorrow,

Allowed an all-embracing sea roar

To rise from the beach up the valley

So prolonged as to be unnatural,

Held up for scrutiny from damp sheets,

Up for praise even,

As if the very frothy waves themselves

Had lapped your garden's edge,

Brining so much saved up movement

From the deep.

Once gone, to return to sleep

You half-remember lines:

About suffering were they in error

Or were they never wrong?

The Old Masters stood

Somewhere on this, you think.

If less muddled, you even

Construct an aphoristic

Philosophy of life.

Caustic reflections and

Sage advice:

Neither a follower nor a something be,

And to thine own false self be true.

Nonsense sounded in an inner chamber

While all around remains dark and hush.

FOETAL DREAM

I dream most of the time,

Dream that I leave this tub,

Step out of this amniotic well

And, carrying a rope and a drooping

Saggy bag, skip lightly into the world.

First sharp sounds,

No longer like one drowned

Hears muffled voices

From a boat above.

Softly, my suboceanic self is

Unleashed from slosh so I push

Ahead chomping placenta

Which tastes like warm pennies.

I heard it all,

The pathetic approbation,

Felt the lecherous strokes and pats

That lingered too long,

Sensed how you must

Live in fear and get by

By living paltry

Versions of yourselves.

My first breath triggered −

This is it, it seems, as

Formless light enters

My leaden eyes.

Now this unprepared entry −

Or exit − is most peculiar

After months of watery rehearsal −

The physicality of it −

The harshness of touch and the cold,

Till I grow old, till I grow old.

GOLDFINCH

When I was eight or so,

We found a hatchling

From a goldfinch nest

On the grass.

It looked like a part of another animal,

Not yet ready to be itself;

A folded, bone-packed

Dandelion scrotum,

Warm in my palm.

I took it home in a box

Checking for regular breath

And offered it

Sloppy bread in milk.

When we came back later it had died

So I prised open its beak,

Placed it under the tap

And let the water run and run,

Felt my chest grow tight,

The soaked bird

Cooling in my grip.

TIMBER

I see the timber, washed up,

These savage ruins,

The debris and waste

Of all the used,

Discarded world,

The empty mussel shells

Filled with black gloop,

The cans buoyed on splinters,

Foam and bedraggled weeds,

All thrown out to the lap

And surge of the voluminous.

Sea-crack, broken rocks

With ginger moss

And that time you

Sat here that lost

Year of grief,

Watching the choppy

Surface with a book.

Some day you'll

See another here –

Some greying flotsam widower

Tossed ashore,

Caked with dry desire and loss.

WINTER BODIES

On that first hot day of late spring

They take out their wintering bodies –

Pasty, pudgy, mottled under

The clear and unforgiving sun.

Look, some have new tattoos proving

Love for offspring.

And now here's a wife; her swelling contains

A fresh demand for inked devotion.

But they're all larger, of course,

Like ballooning,

Comic figures,

Thanks to long evenings

Of corn syrup

In front of the TV.

So they all shamelessly offer their sun-shy flesh to the world

And plunge into the pool with one deft collective jump

Achieving, in mid air, a form of dimpled grace.

DADS

The scene a park on Sunday –

The mums are busy, concerned,

Loaded with wipes and care,

Following their charges

Aware of every risk and edge.

But the dads, the dads are somewhere

And something else;

Checking their phones,

Sighing, pale and permanently haunted

As if some solid macho core

In them had shriveled,

And become a raisin of regret,

As if they'd rather be out on the pull

Or watching a rugby game with a frothy pint

Or in that manly way of doing nothing in particular,

Just lying around exuding man smells,

Flaccid on the sofa like discarded trousers.

ODE TO A SPEYSIDE MALT

Prepare to receive this nectar

Of spring water and malt.

Take it in your palm to warm

Its mossy spirit.

Soon, a sharp wash of pepper

And its ghost flows from lip to nose;

Burning.

A hidden yearning for apples

And the citrus bloom

From the chewable swill, the fill

Of fruit and glorious complexity

Like some late walk

Among dew-thick autumn hills.

Its aftertaste urging another

Sip; a pull for more mouth-filling,

Mouth-fouling pungency

To flood every bud with

Amber rapture.

Now you know our days only make sense

Under a shaft of light

Filtered through a caramel glass

And our hours and cares must be distilled,

Bottled and then so transformed through

Such a sacred seeping.

PORTRAIT OF A CITY

What did I bring back from that

City of layers of old blood

And bones rising to lead-capped roofs?

Predictably, buttery madeleines,

Individually wrapped, from a shop

Opposite a *tabac* that stocked a philosophy

Magazine and '*Les 15 Plus Belles MILFs Du X*'.

Like one of Rodin's figures, struggling

Out of a formless hunk, a pickled man

Sleeping on a bench wakes and passes

A group of tall Dutch teens wilting in the sun,

On the fag end of some delirious stag do.

Clutching water bottles on the

Pont de Notre Dame, the bloom of Europe,

Their three-piece suits covered in white

Dust from rolling around

On the riverbank at dawn.

In the tree-bordered boulevards,

In the avian pride of your waiters,

I can sense how a teacher of the fine

Distinctions among feelings,

Alert to shades of love and taste,

Could lounge here among the lilacs

In the Paris of the mind.

So yes, I have some madeleines

And such pleasure as can be drawn

From the mere hypothesis of happiness.

Vagrants, we'll all keep our torn slice

Of these pale *quartiers*.

GHOST TRAIN

Leather-faced mini-man/woman

With your ballooning gut

Spindly legs swaying

In mock seduction to the pounding rumba

A cigarette paper could fit

Between your oily head

And the tunnel entrance

As you duck, your flowery

Skirt chucked up by candyfloss air

When you toss your tits

Up high our slack mouths

Point upwards till they land

Back in your pink bra

During breaks you draw deeply on a Ducados

And sip a warm beer behind the caravan

For a while you softly stroke your mongrel

With the same veiny hands

That beat children daily with a tiny broom

Did you dream of this?

The cross-dressing

Amid the travel and the dust

The remote towns and their

Powdered beauties oozing

Mid-summer carnality

The early deaths by maiming

The rootless sex and perverse romance

Of being a hybrid,

A macho-pansy never quite

At ease in this sterile land?

But perhaps it's a job like any other:

Make-up, stretching,

Yellow clips on

Like a city clerk cycling to work.

ONE

Durante's poems are

All the same.

He'll kick off with

Some description,

Trying to make

Alien the familiar –

A fiction, with internal

Rhyme.

Then he'll visit his past,

His London days

Of drink and

He'll link this

With present concerns,

To something everyone learns.

There'll be hints of his heroes

In verse: the deadpan, cynical

Tone of Larkin, but poorly achieved,

None of that terse but conversational

Genius and perfect judgment.

Perhaps some failed Heaney too

But minus the rawness.

And then, after some

Apposite or affected alliteration,

He'll go all

Philosophical and,

Round about here,

Try to universalize,

Insert a forced and

Pseudo-profound

Conlcusion. Perhaps

A rhyming phrase

Or two, to end

On a twilit blaze.

PAGE LEFT INTENTIONALLY BLANK

PAGE LEFT INTENTIONALLY BLANK